The Sleepover

Written by Lisa Thompson
Pictures by Luke Jurevicius and Arthur Moody

Tufty the griffin asked Binks to a sleepover. Binks was very excited. Tufty lived on top of a mountain.

Gog helped Binks pack her bag.
They packed her clothes for the next day.

"Thank you, Gog," said Binks.
"Now I am ready to go."

Tufty cooked a pie for dinner.
She wanted it to taste good, so she put lots of worms in the pie.

"I like worm pie best of all," said Tufty. "Do you like it, Binks?"

"Er, I will try it," said Binks.

After dinner, Binks saw the nest Tufty had made for her. It had lots and lots of feathers in it.

"It feels as soft as a cloud," said Binks. "Thank you, Tufty."

Binks lay awake in her nest. She had never slept outside before. She jumped every time there was a noise. Binks was scared of the dark.

Tufty saw that Binks was scared.
"I will tell you some stories," said Tufty.

Tufty told Binks a story about a dragon.
The dragon chased Tufty over a mountain.
Hot flames came out of its mouth.

"Did you get away?" said Binks.

"Of course," said Tufty. "No dragon can get me!"

Next, Tufty told a story about the time she broke her wing. She had to ride a giant turtle across the sea to get home.

"You were very brave," said Binks.

Then Tufty told a story about a monster with eight eyes. It trapped Tufty in a cave. There was no way out.

"How did you get away?" asked Binks.

"I told the monster to count backwards from 500," said Tufty. "Monsters with eight eyes are very good at seeing, but they are not very good at counting backwards. I escaped while it was thinking."

"You are very brave and very clever," said Binks.

"Do you want another story?" said Tufty.

"No," said Binks. "I'm not so scared of the dark now. I feel safe here with you. You are such a brave griffin."

Binks settled down in the feathers and closed her eyes.

"Good night," said Tufty.

But Binks did not hear her.
She was already asleep, and dreaming!